PARADISE LOST

The Unraveling of American Morals

GREGORY TAYLOR, ED.D

See It Through
Publishing

Paradise Lost
The Unraveling of American Morals
by Gregory Taylor, Ed.D

Published by:
See It Through Publishing, Inc.
Atlanta, Georgia 30339
Contact@SeeItThroughPublishing.com

Printed on 100% recycled paper in the United States of America

ISBN 978-0-615-68239-6

FIRST EDITION: May 2012
10 9 8 7 6 5 4 3 2 1

Paradise Lost books are available at quantity discounts when utilized to promote products or services.

Dedication

THIS WORK IS DEDICATED TO GOD, WHO GIVES ME STRENGTH AND TO MY WIFE, MOTHER, AND GRANDMOTHER ON WHOM I RELY FOR EARTHLY LOVE.

Preface

Over the past several generations the very fabric holding America together is steadily being unraveled. This fabric is the moral and ethical foundation that once distinguished the American way of life, a life of liberty, freedom and trust in "God". These qualities of life that have made America great and different from the barbaric and war-like ways of other countries in the world.

America was founded upon a quality that is invitingly sweet but yet, deceptive. This quality is Freedom. There are many kinds of freedom- Freedom of Speech, Religion, Sexual preference and many more. The purposes of this book is to expound on these aspects of freedom as they relate to our values, principles and morality in present-day society.

Paradise Lost: The Unraveling of American Morals is written from a common perspective as a way of touching the inner most parts of man which are the soul, mind and spirit that are common and essential ingredients of a prosperous society.

In our society today, we see drug abuse and addiction, a murder rate unsurpassed by any other country, the failure of our educational system, church scandals and burnings, increasing single parent homes and the failure of our businesses-all touched by a breakdown in morality.

When will it end?

A second purpose of this book is to give certain explanations and possible solutions to these problems. The causes and consequences of this unraveling will be approached from two perspectives - Biblical and Societal.

The Biblical aspect will discuss predictions of present day morality as prophesied by Jesus and his prophets and the aspects of society that contributes to this moral breakdown.

Another purpose is to investigate how the market dynamics of American life when coupled with institutional racism, a culture and family system whose values and organization are in disarray, can effect minority aspirations. Such factors inter-twined with the disproportionate number of minorities shut off from mainstream opportunity will culminate into a ticking time bomb that has exploded into a world of immorality.

Introduction

We are sensitive beings living from day to day on innate primal instincts, logic and rationality. We seek to understand all things but end up missing everything. The Mind, Soul, Body and Spirit, we separate into different entities, but should keep them to form our human qualities.

Education or the mis-education in a lot of cases is what drives an intellectual society. We as Americans- and I use "We" loosely - are in a state of emergency and crisis in the educational arena. It is as though we are in an educational trivial pursuit. We do not have a handle on education. We have one of the best educational systems in the world. If this is so, why are there so many problems in education?

My challenge to you is to ask yourself, "what do I think about the problems"? How can I help? What must I do for my child to receive a quality education? What must I do to change the beliefs of the people I touch and contact each day? How can we as Americans solve our moral dilemma and improve our actions, because we must pass the torch of morality to the next generation? That torch is burning the bridges that subsequent generations must cross , and it is resulting in a society without natural affection, goals, ambition, respect , work ethic and reverence for God.

This book will discuss how the Mass Media, Hollywood, and the general break-down of our moral structure, has led to such low values that it has caused the explosion of Homosexuality, Abortion, Further Institutionalizing of racism in our economic structure and Education. These topics are discussed candidly on a Biblical and Societal scale which give rise to many in-depth questions about our moral values and beliefs.

The Author

Gregory Taylor is an educator and consultant presently employed with the Marietta City Schools in Marietta, Georgia. Born and raised in the small racially segregated town of Laurel, Mississippi , he received his secondary education at R. H. Watkins High in Laurel. He continued his education at Jackson State University and received his Baccalaureate degree in Biology Pre-medicine in 1985. He received his Masters degree in Secondary Science Instruction and his Doctorate degree in Curriculum and Instruction from Tennessee State University.

After receiving his doctorate degree at the young age of 28, he taught several years in the college of education at Tennessee State University and the Comprehensive Sickle Cell Center at Meharry Medical College.

He has spoken or lectured at many educational institutions. Dr. Taylor has an interesting background. Born into a single-parent home along with his three brothers, he had to struggle and adapt to a very hard life, a life that is credited with building his character, work-ethic and religious beliefs. From an early age he knew something was not quite standard with his family. This was even more ingrained when people would treat his family differently. He and his three brothers were born to different fathers which was not well accepted within the community. This family background taught him he could not really depend on anyone but God and his immediate family. It also taught him the frailty of human character. His father did not take an active part in his life . Dr. Taylor's experiences growing up in Laurel, Mississippi sharpened his love of academics, religion and compassion for his fellow man. It is this compassion that drives him to write this book for the benefit of all that read its content.

Along with sharpening his mind, Dr. Taylor holds a black belt in Shotokan Karate. He believes the Holistic or Gestaltic view of a man is the ultimate truth. He believes in balance as does Mother Nature herself. The balance between "Mind", "Spirit" and "Body" is crucial in building Manhood and Scholarship with the Perseverance to Uplift mankind. Scholarship Attainment and Christian Manhood is essential to building a moral society in which all must stay circumscribed with every man with the ultimate goal of building moral character.

Contents

Chapter 1

Effects Of The Mass Media

Individuals in any society learn behavior and attitudes appropriate to their culture, social class, family, sex, ethnic group and subcultures. They learn not only what is appropriate but what is inappropriate.

Many people learn certain behavior patterns and values by accepting Historical or living people as models of good or bad behavior through a process of multiple exposures to animate and/or inanimate patterns of their particular culture. Rather than simply learning a discrete meaning or pattern, the human mind is the continuous observer of and ultimate participant in situations where important others show very small degrees of natural affection, caring, pride, elation, love and fear with regard to some situation. In the end, even some originally neutral stimulus in a chain of cues and responses may acquire a culturally idiosyncratic value such that in itself it becomes a stimulus for a consequent act and a re-enforcer of a preceding action. This entire process may be accomplished largely subconsciously (Wilson).

What is this alluding to? It means that a person can become influenced dramatically by observing others or watching, listening to or tasting inanimate or unreal things. These real or seemingly unreal things can also hurt more drastically than the tangible ones. These things may be television (HBO, Cinemax, Pay-per-View), X-rated movies, rap music, heavy metal, hate speech, drugs in the form of crack, angel dust and marijuana. All these effect the mind psychologically. A pattern unfolds here. You should see a striking resemblance to what is happening in today's society, especially with our younger generation?

The Psyche - It is powerful. The previous statement emphasized " with continuous observance or participation in particular cultural behaviors will cause an ultimate participation in these behaviors subconsciously". This is cultural or social brainwashing that can result in behavior deviant to cultural norms especially in segments of our lower socioeconomic classes.

Society has the audacity to ask," why are young people killing each other"? Why is there so much black on black crime? It happens everyday. A child at the age of three will observe approximately 18,000 acts of violence before the age of eighteen.

One becomes de-sensitized and subconsciously pro-grammed like a robot. This can happen in the most non-violent of personalities, previously unequivocally associ-ated with our young people. It is practically non-existent.

Some of the profound problems that effect our morality are as follows:

Moral Training in the School and Home

The majority of our population is unaware of the many forces that affect their lives everyday. One of the major forces that come into play is the Mass Media.

As Haiku R. Madhubuti states in his best seller- Black Men; Obsolete, Single and Dangerous:

"One of the major transmitters of ideas, images, attitudes, futures, etc. to the average person, is mass media- mainly television."

Jerry Mannered in his Four Arguments for the Elimi-nation of Television effectively illustrates how television has aided in completely altering life in America over the last forty years.

"By the age of seventeen, the average young person will have spent over 15,000 hours in front of the televi-sion, compared to 11,000 hours in the classroom. Thus, a technological, commercial and uncontrollable medium that appeals to the lowest common denominator has a

3

moon-hold on the socialization of most people. Couple such power with all other problems facing young people and young couples, and it is truly a wonder they survive their daily lives".

When discussing the effects of the mass media upon the citizenry of this nation, one is talking about a very powerful medium. Let us concentrate specifically on how the mass media has an affect upon the neurophysiology of television viewers.

According to groups like Accuracy in Media (AIM) and the Parents' Music Resource Center (PMRC), the media's influence is detrimental to the future of America. They argue the media's liberal, humanist bias has a negative effect on the nation's moral and ethical growth, or lack of it. They maintain just as Mr. Roger's Neighborhood, Sesame Street and Barney can teach children to count and read, so too can Melrose Place, 90210 and Models Inc., Basketball Wives, Pregnant at Sixteen can romanticize, glamorize violence and promiscuous sex. As the media continues to multiply through cable television and satellite broadcasting with hundreds of channels, coupled with local and national publications, the issue of mass media's influence will remain crucial to American society.

It is almost impossible to exaggerate the power of the media. We measure power by its effect on those who use it and are affected by it. Its influence is powerful. Soap operas and Reality Television depict a hedonistic life-style that dramatically and grippingly show no respect for traditional moral values, and thus, appear as the norm. Homosexuality achieves a respectability that is questionable, biblically and historically. Divorce is seen as the norm when problems occur in relationships. As you read the following passages, consider the following questions:

1. *According to the author, how is the media destroying America's moral fabric in my community?*
2. *Can I identify personally with his examples?*
3. *Am I falling victim to some of the same immoral traits I view in others?*
4. *Do I get my philosophy of life from Days of Our Lives, 90210, Melrose Place, House Wives, Basketball Wives etc.?*

When one thinks of the questions posed, one could guarantee that most of us are touched, by-in-large with the media. Just think, when you were small, who did you want to emulate? Was it GI Joe, Superman, Mohammed Ali, Kareem Abdul Jabar, Wonder Woman-Who? There was someone you wanted to emulate because you saw him/ her as superhuman, whether in strength, mental ability or athleticism. The psychology of the matter is that we all fantasize about being more than what we are or can be. This might come to light because of a struggle in the realities of our daily lives in order to "Escape". Fantasy can be used as an escape mechanism in order to withdraw. Look at the child that does not have a father as a role model, no home, toys to play with or even friends. Look at the lonely housewife or girlfriend who is having problems at home. Do they not use soap-operas as a means of measuring their life, and how they so much want to be like, or with that sex symbol on television? So, what do they do when that man or woman comes home from work? They compare their reality with their fantasy and most of the time come short on the reality end. Why do you not lose weight? Why do we not talk or make love as much anymore? Hey! fill in the spot with your fantasy. This only exacerbates the problem. Is this you? This problem is paramount today because the younger generation of today does not have the appropriate characters as role-models. They have the rappers, singers, reality stars, certain athletes, pimps on the corner, bitches and hoes among many others.

Although the media producers, whether print, magazine or electronic, continually say," We are only giving the people what they want". They are really fabricating what the media producers and owners believe and advocate, in that amoral, and in many cases today , immoral philosophy is gradually destroying our nation's moral fabric. The media's power is seen in its degrading influence, not only on the nation's morals, but on national defense, the environment , economics, the family and the educational system (Bender & Leone).

There are many examples of the media serving as a catalyst for either antisocial and/or self-destructive behavior. In San Diego a High-school honor student watched an ABC movie on the life of Lizzie Borden, the notorious ax murderer of the 1890's. Shortly after that he hacked his mother, father and sister to death. His surviving brother must live the rest of his life as a quadriplegic. Then, of course, there is John Hinckley Jr., the man who attempted to murder then President Reagan. Hinckley had become obsessed with then teenage actress Jodi Foster after watching the movie "Taxi". In this movie , Robert de Nero played the role of a psychopath who became a vigilante and killed people to protect Jodi. Hinckley was apparently inspired to kill President Reagan after watching the film. (Bender & Leone)

It is my conviction that movie makers as well as the producers and journalists are provoking sexual immorality and violence in our society by continuing to graphically portray sex and violence in the media as the thing to do. Just do what you feel and do not worry about it. They have no perception of the difference between liberty and license. Freedom without responsibility always leads to chaos, and the ultimate end of unrest with this continual rain of liberalism within the media, as well as society will ultimately be destroyed by anarchy.

There are several key assumptions underlying prevailing beliefs about media power.

a. Has the graphic treatment of sex and violence by the media contributed to a decline of morality and trivialized or vulgarized significant aspects of human experience?

b. Has the aggressive handling and criticism of political and economic elites by the media eroded their leadership mandates and led to a general decline in the perceived legitimacy of social institutions, like our churches, schools and the need of married two parent households?

c. Has the media created a popular culture that has steadily cheapened public taste- " sitcoms" and soap-operas instead of Shakespears, Duboise, Langston Hughes and Harlequin romances instead of Alex Haley or Gruindaline Brooks?

(Bender & Leone)

In the midst of this, I think we must equate media content with the effects that it might cause. In the light of this , we must consider what people see, read or hear, especially when they are repeatedly exposed to the content-actually has the effects of hope, fears, depending upon the person's own assessment of a particular message. Based upon this stimulus-response conception, I must ponder the following convictions:

1) Violence in children's television leads to violence on the play ground, in schools, home and the community at-large.

2) Sexually permissive norms highlighted in films, on television or books are implanted into the psyche of those exposed to such erotic content.

I also personally think television's influence on people's attitudes and values, especially the socially and economically disadvantaged is based on their selective perceptions of reality. As a result, television reinforces in a lot of cases, the values and morals to the extent they become null and void. Reinforcement of existing low values and morals is by far a common effect. After all, since you continually reinforce one's self with messages congruent with existing interests and opinions, then you continually affirm those interests and opinions.

Defenders of violence in the media say that hostile and aggressive acts-namely murder, suicide, rape and robbery are always happening in the real world. Therefore, the images that appear in rock lyrics, rap lyrics and television are merely raising our awareness of and reflecting what is going on in our society. As such, they do not affect our behavior one way or the other.

Opponents take the opposite view. They say the media not only tells us what other people are doing, it also presents us with "models" of violent behavior. By showing us violence is an acceptable part of human behavior, the media lets us know it is all right if we are violent. Perhaps the role of the media is somewhere between the two, but I agree with the latter. Just look around you today and ask yourself," what is the major propellant of amoral or immoral thinking and action today". I would be willing to wager ten to one your opinion would be the influence of mass media but, we must also be realistic in that this is not the only influence.

Chapter 2

THE INFLUENCE OF HOLLYWOOD

Redefining or defining our society is a very hard job today because there are so many different views of what constitutes a "normal" society. Group after group are giving their prospectus of what constitutes normality. The transmission of that message is not a haphazard media play with our minds. It is a well thought out transmission of messages from Hollywood with the ability to redefine what constitutes normal behavior in society. The popular culture now consumes such a large proportion of our time and attention that it has assumed a dominant role in establishing social conventions. The fantasy figures who entertain us on our television and movie screens, or who croon to us constantly from our radios and CD players, take the lead in determining what is considered "hip", and what will be viewed as hopelessly weird. In every society, ordinary folk have been able to cultivate a sense of style by grasping the airs of the aristocracy: in this stubbornly democratic culture, the only aristocracy that counts is the world of "celebrities who appear on the tube and in the tabloids" (Medved). Imagine what might happen had some suburban fourteen-year-old independently decided that she would start wearing lingerie as outerwear; she surely would have been ridiculed by her peers and perhaps sent by her worried parents to consult a therapist. The fact that it was Madonna who launched this fashion folly made all the difference, the practice of wearing a black studded bustier in place of a blouse achieved instant legitimacy across the country. (Medved) This is the type of reveling media play that contributes to the delinquency of our ever impressionable children. What is puzzling the professionals in the study of child psychology and the public at-large is that it seems to have caught on like wildfire. With such tempting sights for the senses of the mind there is no wonder our young ones are experimenting with crime and sex.

There was a case where a 14 year old youth killed a 6 month old baby because he was bored and there was nothing else to do in his hometown, or the case where a mother drove her two sons in a lake still in their seat belts because she could not stand the pressures of life. Oh! I do not want to forget the case in inner city Chicago where a mother threw her newborn baby from an eight story window crushing it's fragile body on the cold hard concrete because she was tired of it crying. I can go on and on. As a rational thinking human being ,I ask myself," why such violence"? Why must we resort to killing as the first alternative to our seemingly simple problems? To answer these puzzling questions I would like to start with the young man who killed because he was bored. Hell!! get a real job that will build values and principles such as good work ethics. As far the mother who killed her sons, just go and see a counselor of some kind, talk with a friend, preacher, count to 1,000 if you have to, but you do not kill your own flesh and blood because you can not handle the daily rigors of life. She even had the option to give her sons to their father, but in today's society the man has been reduced to just an object of fertility- a sperm bank, or financial bank if you will. Now, for the woman who just dropped her baby from the window, well she just needs her behind torn out of the frame. What do you think?

Chapter 3

HOMESEXUALITY

BIBLICAL PERSPECTIVE

The aforementioned problems in chapter two are the problems we face in our "civilized society". This is just the tip of the iceberg. There are others like Homosexuality. Now, this is a huge dilemma. We are trying to make it a legitimate lifestyle now. Hmm, just where are we headed? It seems our society is regressing. Contrary to what the experts are saying, there is an interesting explanation to this problem. At this point, I would like to point to a biblical perspective.

THE BIBLICAL PERSPECTIVE- I pray, Oops! I know that I am going to touch some soft spots here. The bible, as a text, or divine word is the most accurate of books as a historical record. I would at this time like to introduce the biblical records that relate or shed light on these problems of society. Let us look at the violent crimes, homosexuality and other carnage of our morality.

The bible clearly states that man, as he gets smarter, will surely get weaker, with the loss of natural affection towards his fellowman (II Timothy 3:3). What is right will become wrong in the end days (II Timothy 3/ Isaiah 5:11-25) ; and his flesh will burn within towards the same sex dishonoring their own bodies. Likewise also the men, leaving the natural use of the woman, will burn in their lust one towards another; men with men working that which is unseemly (Romans 1:27).

Look at how we are taking prayer (GOD) from our schools and every facet of society. And even as they did not like to retain God in their knowledge; (Roman 1:28)

Rulings by justices during the 1940s and 1960s brought government into direct contact with religious life in the United States. In Everson vs. Board of Education (1947), the court sharply defined " the separation of church and state" In effect, the majority of justices in contradiction to the beliefs of the founding fathers misinterpreted the con- stitution. They said the basic document guaranteeing our freedom requires us to keep God out of government and public life. That decision made it easier for those seeking to remove the influence of Christian faith from schools and other public sectors (Bright). Immoral vanities like homosexuality and the lack of a spiritual foundation make a combination for certain destruction.

The reality of God seems far removed from everyday life. As a result, it has become all too easy to become influenced by the incessant onslaught of secular attitudes in movies, television, advertising and daily peer pressure. Homosexuality is on the move in modern-day society. We see it in every level from politics, religion, custody cases in the home and more generally in our communities. As homosexuality increases, it seems to correlate with the increase incident of "Gay Bashing" which is a phenomenon that is on the rise in a lot of our major cities. Some questions might arise at this point," why should they have rights"? Well, they are human and have certain rights granted to them under the constitution . Let us look at some of these issues relating to homosexuals and homosexuality. But first we must look at some of the situations that cause a rift between homosexuals and heterosexuals.

There are certain aspects to the whole phenomenon of homosexuality that make it especially difficult to handle. The societal beliefs that it is biblically wrong from a moral stand point. The incomprehension of the majority heterosexual community towards the belief that two or more people of the same gender could have a sexual relationship. Also the unnaturalness of homosexual attraction in general (Hanigan). The prospect of an intimate physical

17

relationship with a member of one's own sex is often sickening, repulsive and almost unimaginable to the heterosexual person. I would like to delve into the characteristics or psychology of the homosexual. First, there is a difference between a person that feels totally engrossed in homosexual orientation and the occasional experience of homosexual attraction, desire, or even overt behavior. While a particular person might have trouble distinguishing these characteristics sometime in their life, the difference is and can be made both theoretically and clinically clear. A homosexual orientation involves the being and the personality of an individual in a much more fundamental aspect than does the occasional feeling of homosexual attraction or the occasional homosexual act. A sexual orientation defines a person in a way that a feeling or an action cannot. A sexual orientation is a constitutive element of who and what one is, a passing feeling or an occasional action is not or at least need not be, constitutive of being homosexual (Hanigan).

There are constant debates on the psychology or orientation of the typical, if there is such, homosexual. The homosexual orientation has been a part of our history from time beginning as indicated earlier in reference to biblical history. Before giving an opinion on the resolution of homosexuality, I would like to mention some other biblical statements against homosexual tendencies.

The classical texts from the Hebrew scriptures referring explicitly to homosexual behavior are the Sodom and Gomorra story (Gen. 19:1-29), and two from the Holiness Code (Lev. 18:22,20:13).

The two texts from the Holiness Code in the Book of Leviticus clearly states, " You must not lie with a man as with a woman", this is a hateful thing (Lev. 18.22). "The man who lies with a man in the same way as with a woman: they have done a hateful thing together; they must die, their blood shall be on their own heads". This is from (Lev. 20:13). What is expressly forbidden in these texts is for a man to lie with another man as with a woman. Homosexuality, as with any other sin, is punishable by death, and will be dealt with harshly by God Almighty. Homosexuals whether male or female, are human beings and are entitled to their rights. We all are on an even scale there. They are entitled to their rights granted to them by the constitution as long as they do not influence other citizens with those beliefs.

Homosexuality and the issues surrounding it will never be curtailed as long as the minds of individuals are so freely influenced by every flickering spirit of evil in our world. These spirits include luke-warm enthusiasm concerning promiscuity and sex, experimentation, passivism concerning morals, values and principals especially when they deal with younger minds. This disposable generation is left to sew their own imaginations and to reap reprobate minds that spawn new generations of "loose-thinking" individuals. This is the viscous cycle that continuously turn from one generation to the next with the subsequent generation becoming worse and worse.

The "only" comparable antidote to this dilemma is a return to traditional values, principles and morals that can only come from the inspiration and guidance from God. There must be a return to the values we lost along the trail of social and societal growth, and at the same time we must respect all individuals for what they are. We must do our best and leave unto the Lord the rest. This is because sin does not invalidate or overcome God's creative and redemptive work, nor does sin excuse human beings from their moral obligation to one another. The sinner still has a just claim to be treated with dignity and respect, not because he or she is a sinner, but because he or she is and remains human. Whatever judgment is made on the morality of homosexual acts and relationships, there is simply no theological or moral reason to deprive homo-sexual individuals of their human, civil and legal rights, or to deny their human dignity (Hanigan).

These beliefs, as liberal as they may seem are the non-discriminatory beliefs that are the backbone of American society. The right to pursue life, liberty and happiness still has its stringent constraints as well. These constraints are the rules of righteousness God set before us, and until we turn from our wicked ways and seek his face, everything we touch will crumble.

All sin is punishable by death and that includes homosexual acts, lying, vain imaginations, fornication and many others. If you have committed in the least, one of these sins, you are guilty of them all. One must look within to search his or her heart and soul to purify it of all sin. I must ask a question , " is anyone free of sin"? I think not. You can not do anything of your own will unless some higher power has given you the strength. We all need this strength. This leads me to say," we all must look outward from ourselves for help". We all come short of this gift of strength and glory and can not condemn anyone. The only solution for the world is to return to God and his teachings. This is the only way we can save ourselves. This viewpoint is debatable because some of us do not believe in God as a higher power, and that is another topic . In the decade of the nineties and two thousands, American society is liberal on many topics that once were taboo. One topic that comes to mind is abortion . This is one topic that volumes of books have been written.

Chapter 4

Abortion: The Right to Life

Opposing Viewpoints

In our modern-day society where everything goes, we have accepted almost everything as the norm in and what was once wrong is now accepted as right . There are terms such as political correctness, justifiable murders with abortions included, justifiable drug use and the list goes on. Society is being bombarded with views from conflicting sides such as Right-to-Life, Planned Parenthood and Pro-Choice groups. There are roughly four thousand abortions performed each day in the United States. It is the most common surgical procedure in the country and also the most controversial. Abortion affects and involves a variety of people, women who are pregnant with an unwanted child, husbands, boyfriends and medical professionals. The decision to have an abortion alters not only the woman's life but that of her loved ones as well. What are some of the viewpoints on abortion? Based on the knowledge of fetal development, most people agree that abortion should be restricted at some point, probably after the second trimester. It is at this time many people believe the fetus becomes human and has some rights, but others disagree and believe human life begins much earlier at the time of fertilization. These people believe that although a zygote or an embryo can not function as a full-fledged human being, it has that potential from the moment it is conceived. If anyone doubts this they only need to wait 266 days to see what they get (Nelson). Some people believe abortion is never wrong, whatever the reason and regardless of the stage of pregnancy. The majority of Americans believe the fetus becomes a person sometime between conception and birth.

Some say life begins a week or so after conception when the fertilized egg implants itself in the uterus and others argue life begins with the beating of the human heart, or when the embryo begins to look human. Others say human life begins when the fetus is viable, meaning it can survive outside of the uterus (Nelson). This only complicates the problem because technology has advanced so much that a child can be kept alive as early as 2 months. They are called Preemies.

Religions offer a different picture of when life begins. The Roman Catholic Church opposes abortion in all cases except when the mother and/or child would clearly die.

The church further states that abortion is permissible only if it is an indirect result of the medical treatment given to save the mother's life. For example, in the case of an ectopic pregnancy, an abortion is considered acceptable. An ectopic pregnancy occurs when the fertilized egg does not travel to the uterus but implants itself in the fallopian tubes and unless surgery is performed the mother and child will die. So the Catholic Church believes life begins at conception. Therefore, aborting a fetus is the same as murder. Some of the more conservative Protestant Churches, such as the Southern Baptist Convention and various Fundamentalist denominations have adopted a philosophy similar to that of the Catholic Church.

Well, lets look at what the bible says concerning this. Exodus 21: 22-23 states,

"If men strive, and hurt a woman with child, so that her fruit depart from her, and yet not mischief follow, he shall be surely punished, according as the woman's husband will lay upon him; and he shall pay as the judges determine".

This as I understand it, is saying that no man shall take the fruit(child) from a woman's body. Let us look at this in modern-day terms. In the biblical days they did not have abortionist doctors as we have today, but I definitely believe they had certain means of accomplishing this end, just as women today have the means to abort a child without a competent health professional.

Another viewpoint I must mention is that of the Jews. Jewish law clearly states the fetus " is not a person". The fetus is deemed " part of the pregnant woman's body" and the Talmud attributes humanity to the fetus only after the head has emerged from the birth canal. Rabbinical authorities state the time of ensoulment is one of the secrets of God to be revealed when the Messiah returns, and answering the question of when life begins depends on a person's religious, cultural, and personal beliefs. Because these beliefs are so varied, it is impossible to reach a consensus on when abortion should be restricted (Graber). This simply means as people continue to debate these philosophical questions, abortions for women continue to be a viable alternative to giving birth and birth control methods. Some points concerning abortion have been mentioned, but what about abortion itself ? Is it Immoral? One can be compassionate and understanding concerning these positions, but sadly nothing changes the objective reality: Abortion kills babies in their mother's wombs. There is also another tragedy which is a direct fault of our capitalistic society and that tragic reality is that abortion is big business, netting hundreds of millions of dollars for abortionists. The almighty dollar is making us sell our morality straight out the window with no conviction of the heart, no sorrow or empathy . Human life is so precious and I sincerely believe life begins as soon as the egg is fertilized.

Pregnancy is the period for this new human life to mature, not to " become human" because IT ALREADY IS.

I think the government has an important part in influencing the beliefs of its citizenry. Some people argue that changing laws will not eliminate abortions. It is certainly true that a change of heart is more important than a change of law and what is forgotten, however, is that the law is a great teacher. Children grow up believing if a practice is legal, it must be moral. Adults who live in a society in which what is illegal and believed to be immoral is suddenly declared legal soon grow accustomed to the new law and take the " new morality" for granted (Bender).

There is no doubt that a change in the law would further change the attitude of Americans toward the rights of the unborn. There are those who argue that morality can not be legislated and the answer to abortion does not lie in the law. The reality is behavior is legislated everyday. We legislate against going through red lights, smoking in airplanes and other public building, stealing, child abuse, slavery and other matters. The law is made to protect. The law does not ask if I personally believe stealing to be moral or immoral. No one has a right to choose to put an innocent human being to death. The use of ambiguous semantics and euphemisms has been tragically successful in switching the emphasis from "life" to "choice", so that those who are trying to defend life are accused of trying to deprive people of choice. The argument then becomes in a pluralistic society, what authority do you have to deprive me of my reproductive rights? Reproductive rights, however, are not the issue: killing human beings is.

American laws deny the right to kill innocent human beings or even various "endangered species". Why is it "un-American" to argue the rights of an unborn child that depends upon its parents to protect its life. The choice is clear here in this state of morality. Whether pro-choice or pro-life, the choice should be made prior to the sexual act itself. To lie on your back and be responsible for the outcomes, or not to lie down at all. We must take the responsibility God has given to use naturally. God said " Go forth and Multiply" and we will do that naturally. It is a natural thing, but we must take charge of this responsibility and hold ourselves morally accountable for our actions. The fabric of America is becoming unraveled without a shadow of a doubt. It is seen everyday, and it is battered into our heads on the evening news. We cannot go without a waking moment when it is not drilled into our heads. If our present situation is to change we must regain our spirituality and connection with our creator. It saddens me deeply to engage in writing on such a subject as abortion and homosexuality. It saddens me when I think of an innocent life being suctioned and cut into many pieces in the only warm and comfortable environment it knows. To suddenly and unrepentantly get snatched and pulled upon by cold instruments must be unimaginable pain. The child will never taste an ice-cream cone, play in the park and run around care-free. I think it is wonderful to have an innocent child of any race look at you and smile because that is the closest thing to actually seeing God's smile.

"THOSE WHO DESTROY MY INNOCENT CHILDREN WILL DIE", SAYEST THE LORD. "DO NOT HINDER THE LITTLE ONES FOR THEY ARE MINE TO PROTECT AND VENGEANCE IS MINE" SAITH THE LORD.

I am so saddened here because we call ourselves civilized people. We are civilized hypocritical fools. How can a civilized person slaughter an innocent child and throw it's body down a drain pipe like it is trash into a sewer, dumpster or incinerator? To have a child mature to it's fruition and insert a cold instrument of death into the back of its skull and pull its brains out is barbaric indeed. This is called partial-birth abortion and it is performed to keep a certain life-style and we camouflage it as pro-choice. I will pray for their forgiveness.

Chapter 5

THE COLOR LINE

What are some other causes of immorality or amorality? Lets look at morality in a different light . I would like to discuss it on a race by race basis because the United States is definitely a multiracial , multicultural melting pot. I want to be very careful here not to seem bias for one race or another. I do not want to race bash and seem insensitive without condemning any race. I would like to discuss some very sensitive points.

I will discuss the Effects of the White Majority on the Economic Deprivation Of Blacks in America and how this affects their morality.

In this era of space technology, lasers, computer technology such as the World-Wide Information Highway, and Economic World Trade, one would think with such technology, economic deprivation of any kind would not exist. Well! it does. There is the practice of redlining where big banks mark certain sections of a city to deprive people, mostly blacks of loans. There is still discriminatory practices in housing and real estate, government and our court system. What can economic deprivation do to the psyche of an African- American, especially the male, which economic deprivation targets here in Amerika? Let us look through the eyes of the typical black male, which I hesitate to use typical as a term to define a black male because if you are highly educated, white-collar or blue-collar in Amerika, you are still Black.

The education I received was very good, but somehow different than any of my white counter-part's. The common denominator I absorbed after many years of education was that I am inferior, lacking in intelligence, a victim and you know what, I began to see the world through the eyes of a victim. I feel like a stranger in my own land.

The bridges of education are continually being undercut by the white majority. This type of mentality can spawn a "Defeatist mentality" with an attitude of no hope. This has sparked the "No Hope" attitudes that is exhibited in our young people today. It sparks moral decline on every level of society, especially minorities. It is especially exemplified in our Generation X. They say they have no hope for the future because they are so beaten down, spat on, cursed at and blamed for almost every social ill. Their spirits have been broken. They have no natural affection , respect or love for themselves or anyone else. They would easily maim or kill you for just the fun of it. Look at Amerika, it is happening. We cannot blame drugs, dysfunctional families or the media alone. There are many variables that contribute to delinquency and other anti-socialistic attitudes. I know this because I have experienced it in my everyday life. One's drive to succeed can be doused by the constant incessant rain of discrimination and racial discourse, and it seems as if throwing your hands into the air would be a lot better than getting persecuted. Spending my childhood in Mississippi opened my eyes to these different situations. I had no permanent male figure to teach me how to be strong and upright, I was continuously told I could never amount to much as a child from white teachers who were trusted with molding my mind for the future. This seed was planted and watered by institutionalized racism which broke my self-esteem and pride in my people. I did not understand this growing up in rural Laurel, Mississippi . I put the pieces together very rapidly because I did not want to slip into the mentality that I was just another little black boy in this foreign land called Amerika. How does this affect a young black male and make him feel disenfranchised economically from mainstream America? Well, one of the tragedies of Black life in Amerika is that too may black people never acquire insight into their own existence. We do not know who we are, where we came from nor where we are going.

This confusion and identity crisis is one problem at the core of our ignorance. This is the land where genocide was committed against many people around the world; where New York was purchased with beads; where the Indians were lied to and sent blankets, as gestures of friendship, impregnated with the chickenpox virus; where the abnormal defines normality. We are the products of a slave history, slave mentality and a slave life that is meshed with the Eurocentric view of life and this has culminated into a deeper alienation from our history and identities (Madhubuti).

This history, for the most part, was written and disseminated by our white conquers who had one aim in focus, to keep us ignorant, barefoot and enthralled in his way of life. They created in their politics, science, arts, economics, education and religion a rationale for our continual destruction. This Eurocentric rationale provided the intellectual and "moral" basis for taking over the world, ask yourself,after 400 years of slavery has it really gotten any better? I think Yes and no in a myriad of ways. This affects the young black male because in the economics of Amerika he is left out of the equation. He knows the system is geared for him to only receive the crumbs from the corporate lunch tables of this capitalistic society. This is one of the main reasons the drug culture is so appealing to young blacks. They have been left out of the "mainstream" and forced to live in the "sidestream".

We have billion dollar industries in the black community: the church, drugs and consumerism. The black church is the main spiritual and moral institution. It is not viewed as a business because it does not generate much economic income. Drug profits however are different. Drugs are driving the black subculture in many ways. It supports families, cultural dress and identity within the black communities. However, the damage to the black community is astounding. The drug culture continuously takes from the black community like a parasite and does not return much. It is a parasitic relationship instead of a communalistic relationship in which black people as well as other minorities will not develop autonomy without a financial base that initiates and provides for the communities' creativity and resources.

The destruction of blacks start at birth, intensifies during childhood, accelerates during the teen years and is finalized in adulthood. Even the most naive understanding of European-American history should lead one to the conclusion that Europeans "as a collective whole", have left scars and destruction on all of the races of people they have visited. WE LIVE AMONG THE CHIEF KILLERS OF THE WORLD (Madhubuti).

They will visit you by day with their "Cross" on their shoulders and talk with you to soften your spirit. They usually will send their religious leaders to do this. Then by night their soldiers will come with that same "Cross", but it will be turned upside down in the form of a sword. Symbolically , a sword and a cross look just alike but the only difference is they are opposites. A cross is a sword turned right-side up and a sword is a cross that is up-side down. Therefore, in Amerika, blacks are still involved in the establishment of significant firsts. Blacks are first jailed, first killed on death-row and in the streets, first under-employed, first fired, first confined to mental institutions, first imprisoned without proof of guilt like in the O.J. Simpson case, first lynched as in the many cases in Mississippi jails, first involved with drugs and alcohol, first mis-educated, first denied medical treatment, first in suicide, first to be divorced, first denied normal benefits of this country, first to be blamed for "Black" problems- We are the first victims. Most black men know this and seek a compromise with " The System". Some feel money and/ or political clout within the system is the road to "cope" and others think that education or special gifts or talent is the compromise. However, most blacks, especially black males, by the age of their mid-thirties understand such powerlessness and establish a working existence. This compromise, coping and just existing a lot of the time can be so frustrating.

In the light of this so called frustration, what would you suppose whites might think about this situation? Well, lets see if we can get into their heads and draw a mental picture of what might transpire. What are the questions that might arise?

1) *Why do blacks always blame their problems of life on other people whether it be Jews, Whites or any other race.*

2) *If they have the same mental capacity, why can they not compete with Whites or Asians on certain standardized tests like math. Math is a subject that is not biased socially, or intellectually but requires aptitude or mental capacity.*

3) *Why do blacks stand on the corners all day instead of looking for a job or actually working on a job?*

4) *Why do they concentrate on having a nice car with a big radio instead of having a stable family with a father and mother to raise their children?*

5) *Why do they always want a handout?*

These are just some of the questions posed by whites. It was stated earlier these situations whether they are real to the person or perceived by other races, no matter what race, can hurt ones self-esteem. This type of mentality can and will break down the moral fabric of a person to an almost animalistic level.

INTERVIEWS

I interviewed several white couples and asked them some in-depth questions that are considered generalizations or stereotypical questions of minorities in general.

The questions are as follows:

Question 1) Hearing about the stereotypical beliefs stated above, how can these views alter your concept about your own self-esteem, work ethic, values or principles held?

The response given was psychologically typical of what might be expected of couples that are a part of the majority. They responded with the statement that you become desensitized to the plight of minorities because you hear about "their" problems or complaints so much that you stop listening and caring. Basically there was no affect on their morals, principles, work ethic or self-esteem but on the same token, when it comes to quotas and hiring practices it gets more critical. One couple said they believe quotas and other special hiring practices are artificial stimuli because it makes them more protective. They feel the token minority does not deserve what he or she receives because it is based solely on race and not merit. Animosity gains a foothold on their psyche from the beginning. The basic instinct of survival and protectionism is ingrained. Economics can affect one's outlook on other races and cause you to treat them differently. In other words it can cause premeditate behavior. I like to call this the pre-meditated response mechanism. This type of psychological state can cause people to drastically change their behavior and in some cases become violent. Psychologically this is a simple survivalist behavior. The person feels vulnerable, violated and cheated in some way and feels like something has been taken from him or her that is rightfully theirs. Most whites feel the playing field is a lot more even now and these special privileges are not necessary. They feel the minority population is better educated and have more opportunities to become educated. Whites ask themselves, "why is the minority population not taking advantage of all these opportunities"? I ask myself these same questions and personally do not believe the playing field is even by a long shot because "Good ole-boy Politics" is still practiced every where in Amerika. I do believe too many minorities want something for nothing and lean too much upon the past hardships their race has endured. Blacks continually use the "Blood" of their fore-fathers as an excuse to receive retributions. My opinion is that blacks need to leave the past alone and try to improve themselves through the many opportunities provided in America. We will not do it as long as we think we can play the race card and get a handout. Look at the welfare system and what it has done to the African-american community, the economics of America, the psychological and social fabric of Amerika. They have fallen to an all time low. I see it as an educator in the public schools. Our black children are horrible. We have a generation of throw-away kids and it is not their fault. It is not that they have little morality, but they have none at all. This is an Amoral society and it goes to the core of the very inner fabric that has kept Amerika on top for so long. We have not passed to subsequent generations the knowledge of our fore-fathers and parents . The rights and the simple satisfaction of enjoying life and the pursuit of happiness is what they died for. This pursuit has become a pursuit of beating our fellowman to the punch, making the hit, the deal, the kill before the next man, woman, and now child beats you to it. " Makes you wanna holla". Also some whites believe that morals and values can not be legislated. They believe this must be nurtured through basic family values in the home. I agree with this to a certain point, but I also believe the starting point can be initiated from the White House and Government which, I sincerely believe, sets the pace for the rest of the country, because they do this by passing laws that affect us all. These laws affect the way we think, live and plan our lives. An appropriate example of this was when the Republican Party started exercising its leveralistic attitudes by relaxing such historical legislation as civil and equals rights laws. They started the new wave of Affirmative Action crackdown that gave certain intellectuals the cue it is alright to express their opinions publicly through political views and best selling books such as the Bell Curve. These actions reignited the fire over intellectual abilities between blacks and whites and also the issues against special topics in society such as homosexuals, criminals, capital punishment and partial-birth abortion. Other Supreme Court decisions that affected our values were children's rights and separation of church and state, the exclusion of crosses and pictures of Christ on government buildings. High profile murder cases were big issues. The decision in California concerning the man who shot and killed a teenage graffiti artist, or the release of a New York man for shooting four teenagers because he thought he was in danger was a media biggy. These decisions affect our ethical mentality.

Question 2) Do you think Good-Ole Boy Policies still exist?

Overwhelmingly yes: Some of the interviewees were from northern cities and they were surprised to see it still so strong in the South. These were the same couples who stated minorities have an equal footing in society now. They openly admitted it is very hard for them to get into that inner circle because they were first, not from the South and they did not fall into the click of these people. Click meaning the social gatherings, lunches and parties. Today this is called networking and even though they worked with these people they still could not get into their little club. They expressed this type of action will keep a person locked into the past. Good-Ole Boy politics will keep the cycle of intolerance going not only in society but the tightly knitted workplace where big-time business decisions are made. We see the consequences of these types of decisions everyday in the business world. When business procedures of our national banks allow practices like the withholding of contract awards to the minority contractors for Olympic buildings in Atlanta, over-pricing of homes in certain neighborhoods to discourage minorities ,and the scandals in big business. Ask yourself, do I see this happening in my town or community?

Question 3) What do you think of Stereotypes?

The response here was also typical. Most thought that stereotypes have a basis in truth, but is twisted at some point.. They feel most people, black and white, see a trend develop and generalize it to a particular race. Stereotypes are used to categorize in the wrong way and it limits the perception of people and also heightens the anxiety and distrust of other races. There is not much to say about this response except that I agree with it. The generalities and stereotypes we attach to each other especially blacks and whites must stop and we must act upon the facts rather than the fiction. I ended my interview with a very frank question.

Question 4) What are your honest opinions of the Black Male Figure?

Most couples said they were threatened by the black male and did not really know why. As far as being intimidated by the physical presence of black males, both white males and females fell into the same category. They fear blacks that travel in groups especially if they dress in a hip-hop fashion. The white male seemed more intimidated and threatened when it comes to the job situation. I think this is due to competition and protectionism rather than a racial issue. When it came to physical fear of the black male there was really no understanding of why they had the fear, but they did say they do not feel they could relate to the black male , especially the teenager. Violence was dominant in their responses. The responses given signified the respondents were confused and actually misunderstood the black male figure based upon insufficient information. The information they received from friends and associates helped reinforce the information given by the media, whether television or newsletter. Most couples did not have much contact with blacks other than the workplace and in their respective neighborhoods they virtually had no contact. The neighborhoods have blacks but there is no serious bonding or communication.

In our society where de facto segregation is a fact of life, it cripples relationships between the races even through it is a voluntary separation. When a house voluntarily separates it will surely fall, and the value systems that exist in the individual races will pass from generation to generation without the experience of contacting other cultural, ethical and social belief systems of others. This limits our tolerance, heightens anxiety and freezes the expectations we have of other races. This is a limiting factor in the United States today and it will continue to breed ignorance, intolerance and fear in the American fabric of race relations. The positive statements that illuminated in my conversation were of how the black male can improve the plight of his people.

"He must accept his responsibility as the leader or head of his race and take the burden from the black woman's shoulder in the area of the family structure and social institutions that are the back bone of the black community. The social institutions such as the churches and schools. He must encourage education and take a positive position as role model, teacher and just basically taking advantage ,as much as possible, of the opportunities provided today."

These interviews solidified my beliefs there are real fears in our society that need immediate attention. These needs are just as real as AIDS. We need to stop with the rhetoric and intellectual trivia and, put up or shut up. There is a need to act because I would rather see a sermon than to hear one any day and I would rather one walk with me than just to show me the way. I understand society well as a black male surviving in Amerika because I have experienced the discrimination, intolerance, stereotyping and other ills, and being a black male I have light years of ignorance to overcome. Blacks are at the crossroad and must find answers to questions we are yet to understand. How can blacks concretely make good decisions when they are ignorant of their history, culture and contributions to the world? And you know what?, a lot of us do not even care. This reminds me of a situation in my class when I was lecturing on black history. The white kids knew more about black historical figures than the black kids. I had one black kid even ask " Why do we have to learn this junk"? Now, we are talking about black history here. Truly, this is a child that is (sincerely ignorant and comfortably stupid). This incident caused me shame because I saw myself in this kid. Most of us (blacks) want to have the car, house, cloths and have the opportunity to go to a party and this is all we want. Look at blacks today. Humph! We have no political power, we hate one another, we murder each other at a higher rate than any other race, we distrust each other and cannot work together. If blacks were to form an assembly line to make a good hot dog, they could not pour catsup and mustard without criticizing or degrading each other . The race is in pitiful shape. We love mediocrity, just making it on our nine to five hair styling job and do not invest our resources to prepare for the future. Blacks definitely will not save money for the children of tomorrow to improve their economic plight in the future. They do not recycle their money in the community, but rather give it to someone else or just spend it, flash and trash it. Billions of dollars are spent on barbecue sauce, make-up, and hair relaxers, but the black colleges, churches and children are under supported. Blacks always manage to turn it around and say the white folks are discriminating against them, and maybe so, but accountability starts at home with your own people. Blacks complain about white country clubs, golf clubs, universities and other establishments, but they have money. Can Blacks not get together and have these facilities in cities such as Atlanta, Chicago, Detroit, Baltimore and other metropolitan cities? Blacks want to be legitimized by making whites accept their money so they can be psychologically satisfied their money is just as green. To tell you the truth, it is not discrimination that builds facilities such as these it is called togetherness and self-help with pride within ones community. Blacks have to learn this and maybe they will have these different facilities that compliment their rich culture and family values, but until then , they will continue to face adversity and come short of these goals.

Chapter 6

Desegregation

An Impetus of Black Moral Decay

For years the black community held together throughout American history and prided itself upon the high expectations of its membership- its young people, scholars, writers , poets , musicians and scientists. They all held very high aspirations and standards. The topic of desegregation is a very touchy topic within Amerikan society from the standpoint of when it was done, how it was done, where it was done and most profoundly , why it was done.

How does desegregation fit into the moral equation? Well, it must be clear why segregation was so monumental in holding the fabric of the black community together. Blacks for a long time depended upon themselves for uplift in their lives because they had no one else. They looked to their leaders in the community that usually consisted of the Teachers (education), and Preachers (church) for guidance and leadership. They had their own colleges and universities that did not teach racism, but racial pride by uplifting black history, culture and socialism. There were so many positives of segregation, but let me remind you, there were also negatives. I do not want to give the impression that desegregation was all good. The family was the impetus for racial pride. The phrase "It takes a Whole Village to Raise a Child" was actually practiced because your neighbors were actively involved in your growth. They watched over you when your parents were gone, they whipped you when you got out of hand. I mean they really tore you out of your frame, and when your mother returned you got it again. This was one part I did not like when it came to active involvement, but it made me a better child. Where are these characteristics now? I remember when my brothers and I got into trouble and my grandmother was going to whip us, we would try and run because we knew she could not catch us. One particular time she asked our neighbor if her sons would catch us for her since they were older boys. We would run under the house and they would drag us out kicking and screaming like we were going to get kilt (killed). My grandmother hated when we ran, so she would just beat us down good. I will never forget it. She even threw a couple of knives at me once. It is funny now and we talk about it a lot, but it made us realize she wanted us prepared for the future.

The neighborhoods were much closer than now. The well-to-do blacks such as the teachers, lawyers, physicians and clergy were residents of the community and the young kids had role-models. They were not in the white-affluent suburbs. Now these black professionals are moving into the suburbs and the black kids, Hispanic, Asian and other minorities do not have access to realistic role-models. The only role-models they see are the ones on television and the drug dealers on the corner. Desegregation was a powerful dismantling of black moral health and self-esteem. At least when they had segregated schools the students were taught black history, art and culture from people in the community that cared. These people had ownership within their surrounding communities. This gave them a personal stake in their community which develops pride. Now, kids as well as some adults are so out of touch with themselves they tend to lose sight of their precious state of being. They do not value their heritage, culture and life, let alone other people's history. Their self-esteem plummets because they do not realize they are important.

Since the early 1960s, blacks have tried to empower themselves with rhetorical statements such as "Black Power", "I'm Black and I'm Proud", "Back to Black", "Have Pride" and many others. I think the rhetoric needs to be put aside and some action put forth. Minorities, especially blacks, need to have individual love for one's self before there is love for a group because love starts with self-love. They must have self empowerment, and this will not occur until they feel self-pride, affection and in control of their own destinies.

One of the sad facts of 20th century America is most people feel alienated from each other. In fact, at one time in American history black people did feel special. Most did not live in cities, but close-knit rural communities where there was a network of extended families, friends and community groups (Robinson). This is probably why things appear worse today, because there are no ties to one another, no bonds. With the concept of urbanization came alienation, fear, and isolation for many social groups. Now, the whites have tried to solve this problem by creating country clubs, health clubs, self-help groups, cults and other organizations. Blacks, on the other hand, still have their churches, sororities and fraternities, but these groups are less influential than in the past, and somewhat exclusive instead of inclusive in their memberships except for the church. Today the black underclass is isolated not only from mainstream Amerika, but from middle-class blacks as well. As middle class blacks grow older and their parents die, they will lose even more contact with those they have left behind.

The black underclass is isolated into their own world
or subculture. Speaking of their position here in Amerika,
they are almost strangers in a foreign land. All of the preceding statements are social changes that have affected
the psyche of not only blacks, but all races. These social
phenomena can, and will break down racial consciousness
and deteriorate morals, values and principles. This is why
blacks must have "Social Change" in our society before
we have "People Change" and one will not occur without
the other and that is a mouth full. People have fought for
all types of social change since arriving in America. But
in recent history and past history, social change has taken
different roads for different people. Blacks and Whites
differ on their interpretations of social change, because
their language and views differ especially on the topic
of Racism. Blacks see race as all important, while most
whites, except for the most race-conscious see race as a
peripheral reality. Even the most successful black professional fears racial slights or humiliation. They are extremely
concerned about incidents with police, or are mistaken for
messengers, drivers or aides at work. White people do not
understand this. For whites, race becomes central only on
exceptional occasions and collective public moments such
as the Rodney King beating, or when the family decides
to escape urban problems with a move to the suburbs.

Because of these differences, blacks and whites usually talk past one another. Whites locate racism in color consciousness and its absence in color blindness. For whites it is an absence of color consciousness that determines whether racism exists. For blacks color blindness is not possible since race is so important.

With this type of mentality running rampant in our modern-day society we must face these often hidden psychological views and spark debate on the issues to vent them. This process relieves the pressure that builds in a person's mind. There must be an avenue where all races must meet at that fork in the road, and instead of going wholeheartedly one way or another, bring that fork together and form a melting pot of multiculturalism through respect for one another. This is a building process that will take years to achieve and no one said it would be easy. Look at the American people and how we are dividing ourselves across racial lines. This will surely bring this country slowly but surely to its knees as the mighty Roman empire fell. Look at the former USSR and Yugoslavia with their breakup. Most of us in America came over on different boats but we are in the same boat now and in order for the boat to continue progressively, we must all row. Again, I would like to reiterate the "we" in this scenario.

Blacks must reunite, revisit and become friends with themselves and pull off the garb of psychological blindness that is the cause of our present-day slave mentality. Before I close on this topic I would like to say something that struck me odd concerning "US"- the black race. We are the only race that is asked to forget our color to conform to the mainstream. One will never hear about whites forgetting their color to imitate some other race. For instance, desegregation of historically black colleges and universities or when a black politician runs for office. A lot of black politicians run on the premise they are not black candidates or black politicians, but politicians.

I think that is good if the odds were more even in society, as far as Representation in government and political arenas, but it is not. I am not saying we should run as black candidates, but rather we should be proud to be who we are and stop giving up so much of our own identity to conform.

Chapter 7

EDUCATION

CHURCH, FAMILY, HOMES, SCHOOLS, BUSINESSES

Education has been the tool used to pass on values, principles and morals to subsequent generations to come. It is an invaluable means of transferring and acquiring needed information. It has long been controlled by the ruling classes from generation to generation, and only the knowledge that "They" deemed beneficial to all was passed "down" to the commoners. So education can, will and has been shaping our country ever since the "Ole Diluter Satan Act". There are many ways to transfer knowledge and there are many ways to acquire it also, but I would like to discuss at this time the many societal influences that can change the way education is viewed. There are four institutions in our society that must work together in order for us to reap the full benefits of education. They are: The Churches, The Homes (family),The Schools and your Businesses. These institutions must work together in order for a person to receive a full, well-rounded education. Before I get specific, I will give a short summation of how they should work together. First is the Church.

THE CHURCH

The church instills spirituality within us and our children. The church is the number one institution when speaking of morals and values. It gives us the moral qualities needed to be good citizens and servants to our fellowman. Once these values are acquired it is very hard not to follow through with good works. Parents become better parents, children become better children and people in turn become better citizens. The church builds the ideal mind state that carries a person through life. Once a person acquires these qualities, they are equipped with the right ammunition to handle adult responsibilities the world requires. Then comes the Family.

THE HOME

The family is where the values and principles of a person should be attained. They should be attained from the parents who are God-Fearing parents and are responsible enough to pass on good family values, and if the child slips, they straighten their ways. Look at present-day society, the kids do not have any values because their parents do not have any or are not teaching them. So it is not solely the kid's fault, we must return to a strong family structure. Where kids previously had some moral character and values, they now have none. In other words, where they used to be a little immoral in their conduct, they have no ownership of their actions and steadily are becoming more amoral.

Today with the family structure in such shambles our society is falling apart. Single parent homes, where the head of the household is a single female with no support from an adult male. Most of these single females are on or below the poverty line in family income. They work all day and half the night and do not have the adequate time to share with their children, especially males. As stated earlier the children become influenced by substitute parents such as older male figures that are in a gang, dope dealer, their boy on the "Conna" or the drug addicts on the streets. They further bury themselves in delinquent behavior that is perpetuated by society in our Television, News, Music, Sitcoms, Soap operas and Movies. It is not surprising these kids commit suicide and become addicted to drugs themselves because they have no family grounding.

THE SCHOOLS

I think I have just opened Pandora's Box. The schools in the United States are excellent overall, but there are problems in many school systems. This is a topic that will be emphasized from many points.

The schools must work closely with the family structure and churches to not only provide solid education, but activities and alternatives for the youth. The school must first and far most revive the reverence for God. The politicians have done everything in their power to take God from everything public especially our schools which are the perfect tools for teaching values because they contact most of our children in a formal setting. This is not the educational system's fault, but the political climate that is generated by politicians.

Today, schools are at the bottom edge of society and receive all of the bad product from society in the form of kids that have no home training, respect for others, no work ethic or natural affection for anyone. They are dealing with students that are not ready to learn. On the other hand, these same kids know how to make babies, sell drugs which is more sophisticated than a lot of people realize, curse you out, murder and many other things. This is the mentality of society as a whole and the societal problems in which they have absolutely no control. We must remember the school is just an extension of society. This is the case simply because the school is funded by tax dollars, and someone or something must take the blame. We must sit back and think why schools are formed. They were formed to educate the children with skills and knowledge required to succeed in life. When education was in its preliminary stages in America , the people that formed the curriculum stressed classical education . In other words education should be practical and enlightening in nature, but we must remember the student then is totally different than we have now.

Let us compare the past with the future. Education in its early stages focused on developing an educated person who had morals, values, honesty, integrity and a good work ethic. Today the schools are so busy combating violence, drugs, psychological problems, fake learning disabilities and implementation of money gouging programs that they cannot perform the job in which they were formed. The teachers have to be the students' mother because the real mother is on drugs, in jail or in other legal woes. The teacher has to be the father because the real one is either in jail, dead or just does not care, the friend-because they cannot find any in the community because of gang violence. The preacher because their family structure is so out of whack and there is no one to teach them reverence for a higher power. The counselor- to keep them off drugs and the "Conna". The counselors also provide sex education as an alternative for television or the teen magazines that teach them everything about sex except the consequences of unsafe sex and promiscuity. All of this removes the original purpose of the teacher and the process of schooling. Teachers are so under paid it is astounding. Dealing with a hundred and fifty kids a day, logistical duties, meetings after school, coaching and other duties. It is no wonder the average career of the beginning teacher is only three to five years.

Business - Big business is a vital part of America. It is what drives the economic wheel of America. The businesses of this country are the final link in this chain. They continually complain about the quality of the graduates that are steadily becoming a part of the work force. If this country is to continue to function at a high quality the businesses must stop looking at the educational institutions with tunnel vision, in which they are on the receiving end, meaning they accept the finished and polished product we call college graduates. They must take an active part in establishing educational partnerships, scholarships, internship, vocational or co-operative experiences just to name a few. They must also take a bigger financial stake in investing monetarily to not only higher education but also secondary education. This must be an on-going venture that will benefit all that are involved. All of the preceding institutions are very important to the businesses because they are, in their own separate way, preparing the young mind to enter the economic world and become a productive citizen in the community. The businesses are the last link and most have well-rounded and capable people. This scheme is a continuous cycle that depends on interdependence. All of the institutions are co-dependents and if one or the other does not do its job the product (moral citizen) is seriously lacking:

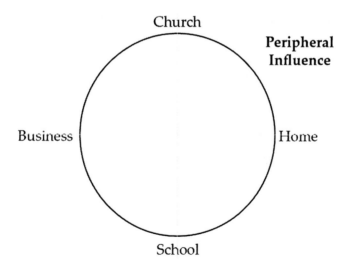

The morale of teachers is so low because of societal, administrative and self-imposed pressures, one would think they needed hazard pay. When I transferred from the collegiate level of teaching to the secondary level I was surprised to see how little respect teachers received from the administration and the parents during conferences. Parents figure they can teach their kids better than you and they try to give suggestions when most of the time they know nothing about teaching and learning. I equate teaching with the health professions. If a patient was going to the doctor to receive medicine, an operation or any other procedure for that matter, would they write their own prescriptions or write the protocol for surgery? I think not . Teaching is also like coaching in a sarcastic way. When the coach is winning everything is okay, but when he or she is losing everyone knows how to coach except the coach, it is the same with teaching because everyone knows how to teach and solve the problems of education except the teachers. If the Lawyers, Citizens, Governors, Mayors and CEOs would let the teachers handle education, I think the profession, and it is a profession, would be better served. With all of these factors affecting teachers and the process of teaching and learning, the learning curve is suffering horribly and it is being passed to the students in the form of lower quality education that contributes to the moral problems of society.

Chapter 8

THE PSYCHOLOGY OF PERFORMANCE IN THE MODERN-DAY CLASSROOM

SOCIETAL VIEWS, BIG-TIME SPORTS

Reflecting on what has previously been mentioned concerning certain break-downs in education, let us look at the students' contribution to this problem and how they are affected by societal views concerning the importance of education.

Students' performance in the classroom is affected by the way they perceive how education is valued by the family, friends, media and society as a whole. Evaluation must shed light on what may cause a student to lower his or her value of education and thus lower their performance and achievement.

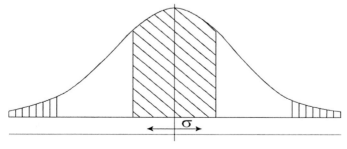

Above you see the statistical bell-shaped curve. This curve has been used to explain intelligence, learning ability and other descriptive variables. I will use it in the description of intelligence. This curve describes the general intelligence of the population. Most of the population will fall somewhere in the middle of the curve from slightly to the right of the mean which indicates they are slightly more intelligent than the general population or slightly to the left of the mean which signifies they are slightly less intelligent than the general population. Now, to the extreme right of the mean you find a drastically smaller percentage of the population that might be in the genius level, and to the extreme left you have a lower percentage of slow or retarded citizens. What this curve is simply saying in statistical terms is the farther one's intelligence approaches the right of the mean the less company there is and it is the same as one's intelligence level falls off. We do not generally see geniuses in society because they are rare. The same with the mentally retarded or severely retarded in comparison to the general population. Look at this phenomena and ask yourself," have I noticed this"? The more a person goes to the extreme end of the curve the less you are accepted by the general population. It does not matter if it is the left or the right, you are marked as strange or crazy because you are not understood and there are plenty examples of this . Where do we place the retarded or severely retarded? They are placed in certain facilities away from society and deemed "unfit" for normal society, if there is such. Now, it is a little different for the other extreme which includes the genius because they are the super intelligent .They are misunderstood and mistreated also but not as severely. The population can not understand the cognitive level of these people so they are "ostracized", "put off", called nerds, crazy, nut cases and other metaphorical terms I care not to use , but look at what is happening in our society. Mediocrity is the " in thing". How does this relate to the student in the school you might asked? Part of the educational reform movement is to place students in the least restrictive environment whether they are mentally slow or bright. This has caused observable problems. When the slightly less intelligent student is "mainstreamed into the class with the purpose of achieving more, due to the mix with average kids, they are automatically marked. The kids in the class know. This starts a psychological mind-set. In most cases that I have experienced, the child does not improve drastically as if he or she was not in the class from the beginning. In some cases their performance drops because of the pressure to perform at a higher level and the peer pressure of their classmates. One noticeable thing, the other class members will accept this person generally because they tend to act closely like them when it comes to classroom behavior. On the other hand, when the extremely bright students are in a class with average students they are tagged also, but they are the Geeks, Nerds, Brains and they are not cool. This psychological process of peer-pressure can be devastating to the overall achievement and performance of a bright child because they want to fit in with the crowd. They will hide their intelligence by not answering questions, have failing test grades and showing bad behavior patterns to become a part of the crowd. He or she is deemed cool and can hangout with the crowd now. This stymies the value that both slow and smart kids attach to education because it is not deemed important in our society. Some of these students never reach their full potential because of this type of societal pressure. We must remember that association causes assimilation. What we need to do is disconnect the politically correct thing and do the right thing by placing these students in an environment suited to their level, but with the right Teachers and Resources. Maybe, just maybe, there will be a cut in some of the dead weight society has ingrained and there can be some justice with the goal of educating them appropriately on their level. These are just some of the internal struggles within education that must be overcome to improve the value system of our young people.

What are some external factors? What about Big-Time Sports? The trend in the sports' world is to forego a college education and go to professional sports. Look at the number of kids coming out of high school pursuing the big money contracts. Society is telling them to skip their education for now, it will always be there if you want it. Just come back, you will have plenty of money to do it because after all, is that not why one attends college to raise the odds of finding a better job and making "Money"? Who are seen in our society as the heroes? They are the big-money sports figures. What our young people see is the almighty dollar is the only thing that is important. You see, this cultivates a negative connotation of values, and education. One can buy friends, boats, homes, jewelry, life and death while the de-sensitization of real values and morality continue to slip literally down the drain. This mentality permeates most all age groups. Examine the problems this will cause society and the professional teams that draft these under-developed minds. The National Basketball Association (NBA), the National Football League (NFL) and other major sports organizations are going to suffer badly. They are getting inferior players in that these young men are not mentally developed. They might be physically, but I sincerely believe the physical and the mental should balance. This balance gives a well-rounded individual that is not immature and trouble- proned. The problems such as defiant behavior, alcoholism, brushes with the law, sitting out games and pouting because they did not get their way, even though they earn millions of dollars to perform their job. One player may earned 20 million and another may become upset because he/she is making 19 million and wants more. When will it end? I am a teacher and a molder of minds for the people who will run this country, but I can not get $50,000 a year with an entry-level degree. Some of these players make more than that in one basketball or football game. What is society doing to itself? Do not get me wrong, these athletes generate money and I think they should be paid accordingly, but 15-20 million dollars a year, please. Policemen and firemen risk their lives every time they perform their duties on the job , but society does not want to give them a starting salary of $30,000, and it are these same policemen who must go to these so called super star's homes to control them for spousal abuse, cocaine trafficking and gun possession. The fireman who puts out the fire on the athlete's 5 million dollar home because his girlfriend or her boyfriend has set it on fire because of an argument. Is it not ridiculous?

This is a subject that really upsets me . Let us discuss for a minute how these sports organizations raise money and I am not talking ticket sells. The politician will raise taxes on vanity products to finance multi-million dollar stadiums, but will not for education. The citizen will gladly pay it for fear their beloved team will leave , and on top of that , pay $40 and $50 dollars for tickets for the games. These same people would die if asked to pay 2 cents more per hundred dollars of their property tax for education. Now these same people want the best education money can offer. My belief is that you get what you pay for, either now or later. You will pay for education now or for prisons later, and the American public has decided to pay for the latter at the tone of thousands of dollars per year for every prisoner. And you know what?, parents will take their children out of school to attend the big sporting events. What kind of moral messages are we transferring to subsequent generations?

The educational system is at fault sometimes. The system will even rearrange the school calendar to make it convenient for students' work schedules, yearly social events like Mardi Gras and so forth. All of these factors contribute to the degradation of our value system. We as educators must adhere to the moral and ethical standards of days past in order to set the right example for our youth. The charge of THE SEVEN CARDINAL PRINCIPLES OF EDUCATION come to mind. To paraphrase them "we must mold a student to be the best citizen possible and to hold the highest standards of conduct and morality, responsible to society and can function as a rational human being contributing to his or her community. I sincerely believe as the great educator Horace Mann once said "The more I see of our present civilization, and of the only remedies for its evil, the more I dread intellectual eminence, when separated from virtue. We are in a sick world, for whose maladies the knowledge of truth, and obedience to it, are the only healing." Horace being a truthful and virtuous man was feeling eminent truth himself. In Ecclesiastes 1:18 it says "For in much wisdom is much grief; and he that increaseth knowledge increaseth sorrow".

One might ask, "how can I improve this situation"? My answer would be to ask the people that are on the front line of education- The Teachers. In our society as I have stated earlier, we operate education under the so-called expertise of consultants, district, local and state administrators, CEOs of businesses and legislators. My personal feelings on improving moral stability, as well as education itself is to not only emphasize the basic skills, but also community values, responsibility and work-ethics to build towards a world class standard in education. This I remind you does not exclude computer assisted learning, distance learning and other modern day technology.

The American public wants the quick-fix , new and trendy solutions. They do not really want to search too deeply into their educational problems because they may make some painful discoveries about themselves and their values maybe reflections of fundamental problems within society. The schools are just a extension of society. We as educators, parents and businessmen must expect more from our kids, and work them harder so they know we expect the work from them. This must be a consistent focus. Other countries do it, why can't we? Japan expects its kids to perform and they do. They do not give excuses for poor performance. They just try harder. Here in America, students develop the attitude of defeat which then turns into self-fulfilling Prophecy. The emphasis in this country on innate ability is startling. It really determines how we view students and subsequently how we teach them. Look at special education kids. We begin to track them very early and set up the educational system to where they never "get it" and are not challenged and exposed to a demanding curriculum. This hurts the student because it locks them into sure failure. This is another viscous cycle in education. Functionally illiterate citizens are produced that are making low quality cars, clothing, homes, computers and other manufacturing products.

While most people are focusing on the school, we

really should reform the thinking of our students ,society and political leaders. The absence of reinforcing critical – thinking, hard work and effort that determines success is destroying the initiative and drive of our students. It allows students to take themselves away from the responsibility of their work. If they do not perform to their abilities it is not their fault, they have simply been misplaced. We must also restructure the way the teacher thinks, their attitudes and belief system especially when it comes to addressing minority children. The attitudes of parents must also change.

While some of our teachers, like many of our citizens, do not believe all children can learn, others pass children for compassionate, but misguided reasons. In the name of protecting a child's self-concept and bolstering self-esteem, teachers have too often rewarded effort rather than achieve-ment. Inflated grades and established minimal standards of performance are given so students can feel good about themselves which leads to a watered down curriculum. This only builds false confidence and drastically under-educated students.

St. Thomas Acquinas said "The poor teacher stands where he is and beckons the pupil to come to him. The good teacher goes to where the pupil is, takes him, and leads him to where he ought to go".

Most of our teachers in America are adequately pre-pared as true professionals, but they have so much to contend with like parents who do not care what happens to their child until he or she gets into trouble . Maybe one day America will wake up from the dream that everyone can cure the ills of education except the teacher. With all of the reform movements, conferences, T.V. documentaries and other forms of communication, the ills of education from the school , the administrators, teachers, students and society can be answered with basic moral knowledge. I do not think it takes millions of dollars to cure the ills of education, but rather a fundamental look at ourselves and the values we hold because values are the highways and by-ways that govern our actions in life. We have for years the results of studies in education that lead us to consider the fundamental aspects of our existence and our Morality. One way or another, society will pay for the inconsistencies in its character. There have been many books on morality, justice and other virtues of society. We must cultivate the character of our children and groom them into good moral statesmen, but sadly this duty has been neglected.

How shall the rising generations be brought under purer moral influences? Certain philosophical questions come to mind. Were children born with good natures that the world just corrupted over time? I think the same sinful nature their parents possessed pre-adapts the children to follow in the course of ancestral degeneracy. This is escalated with the societal influences of television and the value system the child is exposed to. Of all neglected and forgotten duties, in all ages of the world, the spiritual culture of children has been most neglected. The arts, sciences and technology have most generally proceeded, but the fundamental character-building features of man have not. Of all these advances man has not yet applied his highest wisdom and care to the young of his own species. They have been neglected until their passions have taken deep root, and their ductile feelings have hardened into the constant advent of habit. Governments do not see the future criminal or pauper in the neglected child even though they announce government studies on society. They therefore sit back until roused by the cry of hunger from the spectacle of crime. Then they erect their blasphemous head of justice to erect the prison, to arrest or mitigate the evils which timely education and training might have prevented. The courts sit by until the petty delinquencies of youth glare out in the enormities of adult crime: and then they doom to prison those enemies to society, who, under wise and well applied influences, might have been good models of our social fabric.

Who will deny, that if a small portion of the talent and

culture which have been expended in legislative halls in defining offenses, and is sentencing criminals had been concentrated to the instruction and training of the young, the civilization of mankind may have been adorned by virtue and charities to which it is now a stranger.

If animal instincts are suffered to grow into licentious passions, those passions will find their way into the very minute fabric of society. In other words, the freedom of our societal institutions give full play to the passion of the human heart. The objects which excite and inflame these passions abound.

Whatever children we suffer to grow up amongst us, we must live with as men and women with our children being their contemporaries. However intolerable, they can not be banished or made invisible. We must deal with these fallacies of our society with action and not rhetorical political ideologies.

Conclusion

We must face the responsibilities that have been passed down to use through this legacy of life. In a day and time when all vanities of life are taking hold like ticks on a bleeding animal, someone must take action to sustain an equilibrium between good and evil because there must be a balance. There is no balance in society now, and nature does not like imbalance.

In conclusion, I would like to add some thought concerning education that I hope will have a lasting impression on you. Education is your God given heritage, a heritage that a lot of people do not want. Today education is the pearl thrown before a sea of swine that trample it into an obscurity of Ignorance. An ignorance of themselves, history, the world and most of all "THE CREATOR". I call this my Donald Trump mentality. Donald Trump lives in the penthouse where a lot of us want to live in the lavish good life. Now if you take a pig out of the mud ,clean him, give him a little education and put him in that same penthouse, he might like it for little while, but if you take him back to that pig pen, he would most likely jump back in because that is what he is most accustomed to. This is like the children of today. They are accustomed to mediocrity and they accept it as the norm.

FOR THE LORD SAID, "YE SHALL KNOW THE TRUTH AND THE TRUTH SHALL MAKE YOU FREE".

I do not want to make you mad here, but I would like to tell the truth. I sincerely believe knowing the truth will make you free of ignorance. I am not going to preach to you. How can we become free as a nation and stomp out ignorance? We are a generation that has chosen to forget our morals, values, principles and turn ourselves into, not an immoral society, but an amoral one which we not only have low morality, but none at all.

What are your Jerichos in this life? I had many growing up in Laurel, MS. I had no father present in my household, I was poor and no role-models. You know what? I had to take dead men as my role-models. Solomon in the bible whom God said was the wisest man that will ever live. Dr. Benjamin E. Mays, W.E.B Dubois. I had nothing to look to but the Lord . The only thing in my neighborhood were Thugs, Drugs and Bugs. I did not want to be a thug because they do not live long. I did not want to sell drugs because of the same reasons. The only thing I could do for a bug was to step on it. You might ask yourself, "How did you get out of Laurel, MS. and make it"? I used my Four "D" Principle- Desire, Determination, Dedication and Discipline. If you use these principles you can achieve all of your high aspirations.

There are three things that will always keep man from progressing and they are Ignorance, Superstition and Fear. There are also four barriers in our society that will keep us from ever becoming a galvanized nation and they are Self conceit, Wealth, Station and a person's Class. There are also four institutions that must work together to conquer these barriers and they are the Churches, Homes, Schools and your Businesses. They must work together if society is to succeed. I do not know what you have gone through, or what you are going through, but I know Education can bring you through.

There are three types of people in this world - 1) THOSE WHO MAKE THINGS HAPPEN. 2) THOSE WHO WATCH THINGS HAPPEN. 3) THOSE WHO DO NOT KNOW WHAT THE HELL HAPPENED.

Some of you who are reading this book are Educated,

some-what Educated, no Education and some of you Mis-educated. What are your Jerichos in life? We must educate ourselves, our children and brothers and sisters of this world. This is the only way we will see the truth of this cosmetic made-up society. Of all the matter in this world that we see we still only see 10% of the total. It is the unseen 90% that is the most important. Education is the only way to overcome. Hmm!!, You might ask yourself, "Over come what"? There are people in this world that are SINCERELY IGNORANT AND COMFORTABLY STUPID. This means they like being that way. Look at our world today. Look at nature and it will teach you that it is always easier to bring something down than to bring something up. It is the same way with people. It is easy to slide into mediocrity. Again there are three things that will inhibit the progress of mankind. Ignorance, Superstition and Fear. How do these things occur? All of them come from what? Lack of information and lack of an education. IGNORANCE- You know they say ignorance breeds ignorance. This is so true. People passing the vicious cycle of darkness. Ignorance of ourselves, our white brothers and sisters, yellow, red, Hispanic and Asian brothers. Is this your Jericho? You must tear it down.

SUPERSTITION- I am not specifically talking about belief in the unreal or witchcraft or the dark arts. I relate superstition to generalities that are not true-stereotyping, labeling without profound fact that generates beliefs so strong it causes you to have a belief system that is unwarranted and based on here-say like most superstitions. Oh! do not walk under that latter, Did you see that black cat? Someone might knock your teeth out, oh well! let me put it under my pillow because I might get some money. On the other realistic side of superstition or hear-say. Oh! he is black, he is stupid, lazy, unintelligent, uneducable. Or she is white- they will do anything for money. He will kill twenty people on the job if he gets fired. You cannot trust them.

Keep in mind, some people will and have done these things, but one can not say all will do it. What is the answer America? We all have to tear these Jerichos down.

FEAR- Fear is a powerful emotion. Fear!!!! Fear of one another; Fear of not knowing about others' heritage, ethnicity, culture and life styles. Here in Amerika where fear drives racial hatred, discrimination and bigotry, these Jerichos must be torn down. I challenge you, reader to make a commitment to tear all of your Jerichos (Barriers) down. As Horace Mann stated, "the world is a sick world without virtue". This means as we get more and more intellectual and separate our morality and principles we become less and less sensitive to sin. Where is the evidence of this in the real world? In order to see evidence of this you only have to look at the smallest common denominator in our society- our children. The reason why one would start here is that the personalities and characteristics of adults are developed when young. What happens when intelligence is separated from morality?

AFFECTIVE DEVELOPMENT

1. The children use their cognitive development to "Get Over" on the system whether it is the legal system, educational system or life in general.

2. They take short-cuts to everything.

3. They have no work-ethic. They do not cherish hard work and they want everything right now. (Instant Gratification)

4. Lose of Natural Affection for their fellow-man.

5. Criminal tendencies develop because they know no real legal action will take place because they are under aged criminals.

6. They cherish money without cherishing the good moral means of acquiring that money.

7. They do not cherish the value of a quality education.

8. The development of a "TERMINATOR MENTALITY". "I'll be back" to get you before you get me mentality. In other words , do unto others before they do unto you, instead

of do unto others as you would like them to do unto you.

There are many other categories of topics that can be discussed within the context of this book, but I will let them wait until later. I hope, as a reader of this book, you gained a little insight into the breakdown of the American way of life through its value system. We must all work on our basic human values and pass them on to subsequent generations if America is to survive into the 21st century.

May God bless and keep you.

Bibliography

1. Wilson, W. Richard. The Moral State – A Study of The Political Socialization of Chinese and American Children. The Free Press, New York, New York.

2. Madhubuti, r. Haki. Black Men – Obsolete Singe and Dangerous? The Afrikan-American Family in Transition. Third World Press. Chicago, Ill.

3. Bander, L. David and Bruno Leone. The Mass Media – Opposing Viewpoints. Greenhaven Press. St. Paul, MN.

4. Medved, Michael. Hollywood Versus America. Popular Culture and The War on Traditional Values. Harper Collins Publishers. Zondervan

5. The Holy Bible. King James Version.

6. Bright, Bill. The coming Revival: America's Call to Fast, Pray and Seek God's Face. Newlife Publications. Orlando, Fl.

7. Hanigan, P. James. Homosexuality: The Test Case for Christian Sexual Ethics. Paulist Press. New York, New York.

8. Nelson, Joan. Abortion. Lucent Books, Inc. San Diego, CA.

9. Graber, Ben. Abortion: A Citizen'x Guide to The Issues. Alter Press. Coral Springs, Fl.

10. Robinson, L. James. Racism or Attitude? The Ongoing Struggle For Black Liberation and Self-Esteem. Plenum Press, New York, New York.

CPSIA information can be obtained at www.ICGtesting.com
Printed in the USA
LVOW100710040413

327584LV00001B/2/P